The Hornbooks *of* Rita K

The Hornbooks of Rita K

Robert Kroetsch

The University of Alberta Press

Published by
The University of Alberta Press
Ring House 2
Edmonton, Alberta T6G 2E1

NATIONAL LIBRARY OF CANADA
CATALOGUING IN PUBLICATION DATA

Kroetsch, Robert, 1927–
    The hornbooks of Rita K

    Poems.
    ISBN 0–88864–372–1

    I. Title.
PS8521.R7H6 2001   C811'.54   C2001–911065–0
PR9199.3.K7H6 2001

A volume in *(currents)*, an interdisciplinary series. Jonathan Hart,
series editor.
Printed and bound in Canada by Kromar Printing Ltd., Winnipeg, Manitoba
∞ Printed on acid-free paper

The University of Alberta Press acknowledges the financial support of the
Government of Canada through the Book Publishing Industry Development
Program for its publishing activities. The Press also gratefully acknowledges
the support received for its program from the Canada Council for the Arts.

Canadä

The Hornbooks of Rita K is a publication for the book trade by the University of
Alberta Press.

for Dawne McCance
and Bill Spanos

HORNBOOK ... a leaf of paper containing the alphabet, the Lord's Prayer, etc., mounted on a wooden tablet with a handle, and protected by a thin plate of horn.
　　　　　　　　　　—The Canadian Oxford Dictionary (1998)

To Master John the English Maid
A horn-book gives of gingerbread,
And that the child may learn the better,
As he can name, he eats the letter.
　　　　　　　　　　—MATTHEW PRIOR (1717)

No object can be seen, no shadow. The picture's optical framework, made by light, has no foreground, middle and background. Everything is light—even the room. Here a process of perception begins that is hardly describable or nameable. The gaze is now at rest. The constant and fruitless attempts to fix one's eye on something have been given up at last.
　　　　　　　　　　—AXEL MULLER,
　　　　　　　　"James Turrell, 'Twilight Arch, 1991'"

HORNBOOK ... a treatise on the rudiments of a subject: a primer.
　　　　　　　　　　—The Canadian Oxford Dictionary (1998)

The MARGINALIA

Hornbooks

[hornbook #6]

To see is not
to see ahead.
We cannot see
beyond the bed.

[hornbook #10]

Each line of a poem is a provisional exactness.
We write by waiting for the mind to dispossess.

[hornbook #31]

To you, dear reader, frequenter of airport lounges—
even a stand-by poem should tell you where you are.

$\left[\text{h o r n b o o k } \#54\right]$

collecting blue I was
shopping the markets
turning the forfeit smile
into silks and porcelain

$\left[\text{h o r n b o o k } \#75\right]$

Why is it that, without for a moment believing,
we seek out and visit the bones of the saints?

$\left[\text{h o r n b o o k } \#89\right]$

Introduction:
if this, dear would-be lover, is the script,
then you will know why we skipped
                              the production.

THE BATTLE RIVER

MOUND

Archivist's Note: Please allow me. Think of me as a voice without so much as a last name. I have proposed simply to add a footnote, a scrap of data, the slightest anecdote, at most a word, to Rita's dense poems.

Raymond I am, as it were, half technician to her sometimes obscured intention, half lover of the plain truth.

Let me try again. I like the tick and tock of a poem. With that in mind I have examined each hornbook as it comes to hand, here at the dining room table in the house that was Rita's study and her home.

We were, she and I, I should confess by way of explanation, intimate friends.

If I were to give my own contribution a title I would make it "The Poetics of Rita Kleinhart."

$$\Big[\text{h o r n b o o k \#}99\Big]$$

The question is always a question of trace.
What remains of what does not remain?

The unpublished Hornbook #99 may have occasioned, I
would like to conjecture, Rita Kleinhart's refusal, for the
final year of her life (if we are to believe that she is dead), to
add further to the astonishing series initiated by poems #1
to #98.

She disappeared on June 26, 1992, at the age of fifty-five. A
recluse by nature, she apparently traveled outside Canada
only once; she gave only three public readings; she
lectured twice to academic audiences. And of course she
published the ninety-eight brief poems (all of them written
between June 1987 and the spring of 1991, if my intuitions
are correct) that are the basis of her quiet yet enduring
reputation.

Kleinhart was invited, during the late spring of 1992, to visit
Germany and lecture briefly to the Canadianists at Trier
University. On her way back from Trier she paid a visit to
the Museum of Modern Art in Frankfurt and while at the
museum mailed a number of postcards to friends. She was
not seen alive thereafter.

Her ranch in Central Alberta—her house overlooking the
coulees and the valley of the Battle River—contained at
the time of her disappearance neat stacks of scrawled
notes, manuscripts, partially filled notebooks and, yes,
unfinished (or unfinishable?) poems.

The opening of #99 exists in a number of versions, with no particular version indicated as her final choice. On the top of a sheaf of drafts I found two lines on a single sheet of paper:

I am watching the weather channel.
It is that kind of day.

Rita questioned and even rejected ideas of evolutionary development in art. She had other fish to fry.

[hornbook #84]

Why don't you close doors? Rita once asked me, when I indiscreetly left a door open behind us. I was born on a raft, I replied.

I knew how to irk her and at times couldn't resist. Rita Kleinhart was persuaded that her notion of collective biography—the expression is mine, not hers—could not be located in a system of beliefs or a narrative of origins. It could only be located, literally and momentarily, in back doors.

Her fascination with back doors—of houses, of apartments, even of garages and barns and public buildings—announces her interest in collective biography. Her brief but eloquent poems on the subject of the back door speak to and of the pathetic beauty that we create by way of rejection and something that one might call denial. Back doors are, she proposes in her notebooks, the escape from transcendence. They are also the escape from so-called good neighbors and possibly from language itself.

I tell you this because my own recollections, along with the neat stacks of paper of which I have made mention, give the lie to the published poems so treasured by Kleinhart's (albeit it too few) devoted readers.

[hornbook #83]

Kleinhart earned the displeasure of some of her neighbors in her generous attempt to write for them a collective biography. Her announced intention of inscribing in her poetry the ninety-nine back doors that were nearest her own led, on more than one occasion, to her being forcibly evicted from so-called private property. Her response was to write on the back of an envelope that was addressed to me but never mailed:

One cannot, now, be a love poet. Now one can only be a desire poet.

Kleinhart sometimes worked from photographs. She would not snap a picture until she saw a person entering or exiting from the back door in question. The subjects, I hasten to say, survive in those photographs as nothing so much as blurs—surrounded, often, by unintended or even embarrassing detail.

Living in relative isolation as she did, on a fairly large ranch, dear Kleinhart fell prey, along with her isolate desire, to rampage need. Her attempts to *regard* (a verb she much liked) the back doors of near and not-so-near neighbors led to her being labeled not only a recluse, but also a snoop and a thief, a voyeur, a strange bird and, as some of her farther neighbors put it, a nut case.

Collective biography, of course, attempts to locate collectivity at the bottom, so to speak, not at the top. Rejecting notions of the religious or political or transcendental or the Platonic ideal or, apparently, the narrative of love, Rita blundered into the predicament that haunts us one and all. She sums it up abruptly in her lines:

> prairie/rain: do not look now but
> there is a ship on the horizon.

$\big[$ h o r n b o o k $\#12\big]$

Somewhat fascinated by prairie cemeteries, Rita was ever attracted to the bare wooden crosses she found in those small rectangles of fenced sod. She worshiped, in her own way, the peeling white paint, the smell of rotting wood, the worn pathways of ants—and at the same time she loathed anything those crosses might, as the expression has it, signify. It was the stolid, dumb, wooden repetition, from graveyard to graveyard, that fascinated her.

She found that same stolid, dumb, fascinating repetition in back doors.

Back doors are the very locus of discharge and communality. Kleinhart mentions at least three times in her notes a particular occasion when, injured at play, muddy, crying, she was told by her mother to go around the house and use the back door.

What is more precious in our collective biography than
those very things that we elect to conceal or discard?
Discard is the most enduring version of circulation;
discard, not retention, constitutes the materiality of trace.

In her questioning of notions of the unique and singular
self, Kleinhart turns often in her work to the slippage
between the words "I" and "It." On one sheet of paper in
the stack that I have designated the Battle River Mound
she writes, almost confusingly:

> He was standing at my back door.
> It was late in the afternoon.

By the recording of something that was possibly not in her
photographs she permits herself to continue:

> At the back door the assassin
> handed me his knife.
> He asked for a slice of bread.

> At the back door Louis Riel
> asked if he might use the bathroom.

$\left[\text{h o r n b o o k } \#76\right]$

Sometimes I hear in my speech traces of languages I don't remember knowing.

This preposterous statement is scrawled on a scrap of wrapping paper. Granted, our language does unwittingly acknowledge its Indo-European roots. And one might wonder at the impossible moment when, somewhere, somehow, a speaker joined together—let us say—three words. But does not accident precede design?

Kleinhart claimed to be writing investigative poems. What, pray tell, was she investigating?

She writes not once but twice, each time as if for the first time:

> The river of no flows over us.
> Nothing is new.

[in one of the two versions the word surprise is written over the word no, but neither word is scratched out]

I confess to puzzlement. Frankly, you would have to lie down flat on your back in the Battle River to have the water flow over you. The huge valley of that river was not carved out by the piddling stream that it now contains; the outwash of retreating glaciers created what now seems a pastoral site.

$$\Big[\text{h o r n b o o k } \#41\Big]$$

The
apples

spinning

on
their

tree.

Rita was not one to look for connections.

Sometimes, it seems to me, she thought of people as some sort of computer virus that had got into the intelligence of the world. On a draft of this hornbook she wrote:

When I was a child my Aunt Agnes told me not to swallow cherry stones. If I swallowed a cherry stone, she told me, a cherry tree would grow out of my belly. I shuddered at the idea. And yet I found it curiously exciting. Growing up in Alberta, I had never seen a cherry tree.

I would speculate that she had in fact somewhere seen a reproduction of a woodcut from an old book, and in that reproduction a cherry tree cramped into a small, rectangular space. I have seen such reproductions myself. She, however, went on to reckon that her language was freighted with no end of traces that were neither literal nor metaphoric. What in hell, then, I would like to have asked her, were they?

[hornbook #61]

Rita Kleinhart was at work on a huge—and I would say, bizarre—work that ultimately, I am persuaded, caused her disappearance. She held to the conviction that she might so write her poems that she would leave each object or place or person that fell under her attention undisturbed.

Granted, she did not, looking at back doors, tug at latches or twist at knobs. And yet she proposed at one point in one of her notes (though she may have later abandoned the idea) that she would limit her investigation to her own township. A township is, of course, in its own insistent way, a box. Kleinhart has nothing to say on this matter. Or, at most, she drew on a sheet of paper a square full of squares, then commented in the margin: A township is not a box.

I might explain to the unwary reader that a township, as conceived in Kleinhart's home province, is a square of land measuring six miles by six miles, resulting in a grid made up of thirty-six squares of land each measuring one mile by one mile. These thirty-six sections (as they are called) are numbered from one to thirty-six, beginning not from the top left-hand corner as one might expect, but rather from the lower right-hand corner, then to the left, then up a row and to the right, then up a row and to the left, then up a row and to the right, in the time-honored manner of a farmer plowing a field with oxen or even a four-horse team.

Rita Kleinhart went too far, I feel, both with her notions of the nondevelopmental nature of the individual artist's work and with her commitment to versions of the serial.

Things happen, she writes, and then things happen. And there is sweet fuck all else to it.

[hornbook #42]

Ideas of development, Rita insisted, make for a false narrative of what it is to be a poet or person; as a result the house that survived her disappearance is a hodgepodge of so many midden heaps. And I am stuck with the task of being mild philosopher to her estrangement from both the reality of now and the larger intentions of immortality. Being in-between, she should have realized, we cannot ever be.

Rita and I were lovers for four years. During that time we met three times. Because we were separated in age by a good ten years, I was gone from the Battle River country and launched into my own career by the time she published her first poems.

I did, however, continue to correspond with Rita after our unfortunate separation (though my letters to her are, so far, not to be found in her house). In one of her letters she tells me, If you are going to appropriate from your own life, do so with immense care.

By way of retort I penned to her a three-line stanza which I chanced to commit to memory:

Retreating from his own back door
the invisible man stepped on his invisible dog
and, having been bitten, bled red blood.

Her sullen little response was to send me a postcard saying what I had already understood: Listen, Raymond. If you are going to ... Et cetera. Et cetera.

At that point I became a bit huffy. I told her, by special delivery, in no uncertain terms, that I would prefer to be left out of her collective biography.

She responded by writing me a pair of three-line stanzas for which I can only assume I was the inspiring if invisible muse:

> At a side door of the CN boxcar
> the immigrant farmer ate the horse
> he had intended to ride home.
>
> At the only door of the homestead shack
> the immigrant wife called to her husband,
> Where did you pack the wine-dark sea?

I suppose it was unfair of me to be flip in my response, but I responded by writing, I see you would like to see me again.

Her response was a long and remarkably clumsy sentence that struck something of a blow at her own sense of independence:

The loneliness of the poet is so immense I might only endure it by sending you blank postcards from the museum of your mind.

[hornbook #43]

Rita thought of calling her book *Chance of Flurries*. That she elected not to is fortunate, since I would surely propose other titles for her unfinished magnum opus.

We write as a way of inviting love. Each text is a request that says, please, love me a little.

Rita Kleinhart was an admirer of snow. Snow, she remarks, is the caress of impossible meanings. Snow is closure without ending. Snow is the veil that lets us see the shape of the dream.

Rita left two solitary lines that seem to belong nowhere:

A skiff of snow, this morning, rides the stubble sun.
The gosling, holding madly still, accounts the gun.

I, too, have walked in the ribald dark, asking forgiveness. In the absence of the gun, snow suffices.

[hornbook #45]

What is the heart but the muscular, thick skin of an
abiding secret?

She referred to me as the intrigued lover.

Broken, she said, and wrote these lines after that solitary
word, as if she had put down a title:

> He is the intrigued lover who loves first
> his own hands. His hands betray my nipples.
> His hands are scissors that break rocks.
> And yet he is the intrigued lover who asks,
> Where do you go when you close your eyes?

There is a break on the page. Then she continues:

> You of the stalled orgasm, fearing an end—
> I give you nothing. Die by your own hand.
> Love is a pleasure of the mouth. Eat your words.

Surely she intends these final lines for me. She is nothing
if not direct. I see in these lines intimations of her
disappearance; what is love but a disappearing act that
leaves the beholder staggering in blind pursuit? I find Rita
nowhere, and yet I am in her arms when I awaken. She ties
me to her bed.

Her restless words begin, like the lick of snow, their
incisions.

$\left[\text{h o r n b o o k } \#65\right]$

I wrote to her and said, Say hello to Zero, but she wrote
back and said, We met a long time ago, but you don't
remember. That's when I replied, I love you, but how
would you know?

A drunken angel fell upon the chimneys of the town.
A woman in a doorway heard a weeping.
She said it was the whimsy of a clown.

Did Rita write those exquisite lines, or did I?

I have always admired Li Po and Tu Fu. I think of that drunk
man—Li Po?—seeing the moon in the water and believing
he saw the figured, white, round, smooth, cloven,
irresistible ass of his love. He reached to offer a kiss. He
would embrace what he most desired. I once sent Rita a
postcard reminding her of the event. Even now I weep
small tears of my own at Li Po's drowning.

$\left[\text{h o r n b o o k } \#64\right]$

Poet, before I forget, tell me nothing.

[hornbook #94]

"fragments after a fragment." That would be my title for Rita's work. I once wrote briefly, telling her as much. Think of poor Osiris, I added, hacked to bits out of rage and jealousy.

She wrote in reply: "Headset" would be the proper title for your own speculations. Your way of not hearing the noise. You put on your headset and you hear one sound with determined exactness.

She was ever the champion of background noise, a fact that makes her disappearance into silence all the more irritating. Was not her life on the ranch silence enough?

I am reminded of a couplet she sent me shortly after we entered into what was to be a correspondence, and I had the temerity to say our beginning to correspond was a good thing:

> Your life broke its leg;
> you ought to shoot it.

Gibberish, I replied.

Precisely, she wrote back. Now you are beginning to hear.

$\left[\text{h o r n b o o k } \#48\right]$

In the first two stanzas she stands at her back door, guessing where she might put a new birdhouse. She notes the cheekiness of chickadees; she regards the flight of a swallow, unpredictable as it is certain.

Apart, we hold hands. Our bodies become the signs of what it is they want to deny. Only our bodies are unable to forget.

I am reminded of a comment from the bleared, hazel eyes of old _____: Autobiography is not memory.

Now where did that fucking garden get to? Rita asks at the end of Hornbook #48.

$\left[\text{h o r n b o o k } \#29\right]$

Flightless as snakes, we read flatly what cannot be flat. The open prairie conceals a chasm. How does one dare walk through tall grass?

> Surprise, surprise.
> It was surprise put out his eyes.

I quote. But I would like to propose my own substitution for Rita's offending lines:

> The gopher, standing on its mound to see,
> gets shot between the it and me.

$$\Big[\text{h o r n b o o k } \#30\Big]$$

Why do I imagine phone calls in which she tells me I have disappeared?

$$\Big[\text{h o r n b o o k } \#4\Big]$$

The hornbook is itself a book, but a book one page in length. Framed and wearing a handle, covered in transparent horn, it sets out to fool no one. It says its say. Rita Kleinhart seems not to have got a handle on this realization. What she claimed for her poems was exactly that which they did not provide: the clarity of the exact and solitary and visible page. The framed truth, present and unadorned. Not a page for the turning, no, but rather the poem as relentless as a mirror held in the hand.

The framed and confident statement, announcing precept or command; the framed list, offering the barest alphabet and numerals of our lives. A one-page book covered in horn, but not a horny book. The dehorned beast, offering its last sign and protection to protect the isolate sheet of paper and its insistent economy of words.

[24]   ROBERT KROETSCH

[hornbook #22]

I once phoned Rita to say I feel safe only when on airplanes.

I make my living as a courier—or, as I prefer to say, using a word that refuses to wear a disguise, messenger. I deliver confidential documents from place to place, from continent to continent.

While up in the sky I write a few poems of my own. Or I used to. Of course I could not afford to let them survive any landing. Let me tell you, a messenger recognized as a poet would soon be out of business.

Writing, Rita assured me in her absurd way, is not about delivering messages. She dotted in an ellipsis as if to give me time to think. It is equally important, she went on, that we have messengers and keep them desperately busy. Do you know what I mean?

Since Rita left her Alberta ranch at best once a month, and usually to travel something like two hundred kilometers, she was hardly in a position to deliver messages to anyone.

Hornbook #22 contains the caressing lines:

> crushed red shale in my lane,
> rain falling on fallen rain on
> crushed red shale, fire, flood

The long lane that leads from the paved road to her ranch house is indeed covered with crushed red shale. Saskatoons and chokecherries grow in patches here and there, along the lane. Pasture sage finds a place in the bunch grass. Wild roses. A slough with its ring of willows and trembling aspen. But what one sees mostly and simply is barns, granaries, corrals, a ranch house that is at once rambling and severely unprotected, there on a stretch of prairie overlooking the wide valley of the Battle River.

Where would I go? she asked me, when I asked why she didn't travel.

Her disappearance, while in the Frankfurt Museum of Modern Art, puzzles her enemies and friends alike. I have never told anyone that I am certain I saw her late one afternoon on a Singapore subway train, only eight months after her disappearance. She, of course, gave me not so much as a blink of recognition. Seeing her as I did, through a moving window, I was reminded of her photographs of back doors—photos in which, by accident, she more than once captured herself as reflection in glass.

Why did I not try to overtake her, there in Singapore? Quite simply because I respect her wish to remain silent.

During that same trip, while on a 747 returning home from London, I wrote in response to Hornbook #22:

She is poet to her own patience.
She rides the long hours, rounding up
strayed words. Howdy, pardner.

[hornbook #23]

Can there be a poetics of regret? Not likely. Rather, I find in Rita's work a longing for the future. This longing is not in any way utopian. Nor does it hint of a longing for death—which is only a wily variant of the utopian.

Her disappearance, rather, had everything to do with entrance into the world. Only by disappearing could she escape the bonded ghost she had become to her few readers.

By that act of disappearing—and I believe she willed it—she gave freedom to her poems. And further, she freed herself of any need to write more poems. Her existing poems could begin the process of rewriting themselves, as any poems must that are felt to be poems.

Rita wrote a mere two lines [she left those lines—

the patient prisoner
the frittered sky

—out of the published version] on the subject of air travel, and yet those same lines anticipate my entire life. Destined never to land. Confined to air. The prisoner of flight.

Rita would seem in those gifted lines to anticipate a kind of love for me. I can only say, now that she is absent, that I, too, loved her.

I thought of myself, often, while circling this little planet, as flying around her, always toward her. I carried with me her sheaf of poems. I read them and was compelled by their knotted intentions into words of my own.

Now she has taken flight and I am alone on this flatbed earth.

[hornbook #66]

I have to run around and pick a few things up.

The last time I dropped by to see her on her secluded ranch, I found the above note nailed to the back door. Rita made an adventure of driving her pick-up truck into town. She could hardly have anticipated that I might drive two hours from the city in order to share with her a pot of coffee. That she did not feel it necessary to scrawl my name is further evidence of her assumption of our connection.

Poetry itself is just such a surmise. I speak to no one, knowing you will recognize that I speak to you.

[h o r n b o o k #67]

Rita, shortly after her disappearance, began to send back
to her ranch house postcards addressed to herself. At least,
I am certain it was she who sent them, this deduction
based on their content.

It is my every intention ... she wrote, addressing herself.
And then, hardly a week later, she sent herself a message
that she must have assumed would fall into my hands:
What are you flying off about? she asks, on the back of a
card that pictures a large jet with nothing behind it but sky.

Both cards bear French stamps. Both arrived hardly a
month after the provincial authorities named me as the
archivist who would put together her literary papers. The
law recognized that our love relationship had continued,
even if that recognition was beyond Rita herself.

[h o r n b o o k #7]

I am attempting to write an autobiography in which I do
not appear.

Rita Kleinhart, in making this comment on her own
poem—a comment I found attached to the manuscript of
the final (and published) version of Hornbook #7—both
announces and betrays the posture that is the very
bedrock of her entire poetic sequence.

She would, so to speak, deny her own signature. And yet she wore the world in a way that was uniquely hers. She loved the smell of a shared bedroom, the distant calling of cows and calves, the taste of swollen raspberries made wet with fresh cream—even as she claimed not to love me.

[hornbook #8]

Rita is painfully absent when I let myself in at the back door of her richly modest home.

A man of your age. For shame, she once commented, while we were in the throes of our lovemaking. I had, while kissing her back, quietly slipped her jeans well down below her waist and let my tongue in at the cleavage of her perfect behind.

A man of my age, indeed. I was precisely a decade her senior. She and I became lovers on her fiftieth birthday. I was, at the time, sixty years of age, and fit as a fiddle.

Is not poetry a questing after place, a will to locate? I flew, and I was weary of flight. Rita was mistaken when she speculated that I took to the sky under the fond illusion that I might in that manner get nearer the sun.

We were talking.

Do you like it?

Perhaps, she offered, her voice at once light and husky.

I was stuck for words.

[hornbook #3]

How is it, the poet asks herself on the back of a slip torn
from a calendar, that the poet writing writes herself into
the recognition that she is not saying what she wishes
to say?

Recognizing this, the poet moves on, doesn't she? Death
follows after like a dumb admirer. What is the poetic
function of the hand?

> Once upon a time, long ago.
> Long a time. Once upon a go.
> Long upon ago a once a time.
> A time ago upon. A long. A once.

I was trying to tell you a story, Rita. The pathology of
grammar. I had trouble getting stopped.

> Lugubrious as love,
> we love.

[hornbook #39]

As a small child I was puzzled by clocks. I studied the face of the large clock mounted on the wall in our kitchen, and I tried to understand how adults looked at that face and then said to each other: The train is late today. The roast should be done by now. It's time the children took their baths.

The face of the clock was a hieroglyphic I could not penetrate. I studied the slow pointing of the hands from number to number. I had learned the numerals well enough so that I might read them up to twelve. But how did those numerals tell people to wash their faces and comb their hair? How did that circle of motionless numbers tell people to say goodbye to each other and go out into the dark and the cold of the night?

[hornbook #40]

Discomfort, Rita told me, and this over a breakfast of ham and eggs and brown toast and her own homemade chokecherry jelly, is what you look for in a poem, Raymond. You seek discomfort the way you seek dislocation.

By way of smart retaliation—and our fingers touched across her kitchen table as I spoke—I quoted from her own Hornbook #40:

Home is a door that opens inward only.
So how will you get out, stranger? I say
to myself.

Perhaps I was only suggesting, she said, smiling
mischievously, that words are a lock, not a key.

Then how do you explain, I said, not smiling at all, that
every time I peek in at your keyhole, I get a shiner?

Who is this I? she asked.

Your own Raymond.

I can't place him.

I think he loves you, I said. He's probably hiding
somewhere in this house.

[hornbook #77]

The poets of Canada learn to sing by walking barefoot on gravel beaches. This makes for a fascinated listening. A constricted listening.

Why did she not speak of the writing? But no, not Rita— she, the poet, would speak of the listening instead.

I'm not convinced she ever heard a word I spoke to her. I offered her praise and love. She did not know how to accept either. We deceive ourselves into words when all that cries out is the body, wanting touch and taste and smell and sight. Do you hear me?

Words are the fake pockets on a new jacket. You cannot tumble into one of them so much as a token coin. Words are what we are left with by the bird that hits the window.

Invisibility was what Rita wanted. I asked her one May afternoon what she would like for her birthday. An eraser, she said.

My dear, I replied. I am offering you all of me.

You see, until Rita Kleinhart chose to disappear there in Frankfurt, I thought of myself as a poet. That I wrote the poems while in the air, that I destroyed them just before the plane's tires smoked down onto gray pavement, has nothing to do with what I knew I was doing. I was a poet. It was my touching the delete button that made those high poems complete. What I might dredge up from memory now, in order to communicate with Rita's absence, has nothing to do with the poems as they existed above the clouds. Every published poem is its own elegy. What poet is not astonished, reading the mere poem on the mere page? The mere transcription of that other poem onto paper is a calamity, a desecration. Every poem, one might say, is a failed translation, an accidental imposter manu-fractured by the incompetence of a weak-eyed translator sweating in the light of a lantern whose wick is badly in need of a trimming. The wind blows hard. The flame flickers. The sooty globe needs a wiping. The word asshole comes to mind. And, yes, after flying across continents and oceans, while approaching once again this petty, stinking earth, while ignoring some flight attendant or other who cries out incoherent commands, I have rushed at the very last minute to the john at the back of the plane, pushed my way into a filthy cubicle (and during a flight of eight hours the human mob declares itself by its telltale toilet inscriptions to be what it is) and there proffered the scribbly copies of my absolute poems to the sudden, loud suck and the whoosh and the exquisite oblivion of the Teflon shitter.

[hornbook #19]

Rita was accustomed to the deceptive randomness of wind and rain and sky, to the violence and the blinding inevitability of prairie sun. She had an aversion to intentional space.

She wrote on the reverse side of the sheet that contains Hornbook #19:

A patch of scarlet mallow appears each spring in the grasses on the edge of the coulee directly in front of my house. That little patch of orange-red blossoms, emerging on a dry, south-facing slope, is one of my reasons for living.

She wrote in the margin of Hornbook #19:

I have discovered that negligence is a gifted gardener.

Forgive me for having added at the bottom of that same page:

The day they brought my mother's body home to our house for the wake, I went up the low hill behind our house. Rita, I wanted to tell you this. I went to a hollow beside a large round rock, and I curled up in that hollow and I cried until I had cried out my life. After that I was empty enough to be a poet. I returned to the house and went to my room and made a list of the names of the neighbors who came with food and flowers.

In the end, we are defeated by gardens. They know too much.

[hornbook #53]

There in Frankfurt, on the occasion of Rita's disappearance
(and I was standing beside her in that darkened room
where one believes one is looking at a framed painting only
to discover, as one's eyes adjust to the dark, that one is
staring into a faintly lit recession set blankly into a blank
wall), I turned to remark that I found James Turrell's
"Twilight Arch" compelling nevertheless, for all the
absence of an image. I turned and she was not there.

$\left[\,\text{h o r n b o o k }\text{\#}44\,\right]$

[an endnote to begin with: Rita felt little need to travel in
this ravaged world. She once heard me speak of the city of
Coimbra in Portugal and (if I am not mistaken) wrote
Hornbook #44 in response to my claiming to have shed
tears at the sound of a voice I heard without every laying
eyes on the singer.]

1

I am happy in the Coimbra night.
The stars feed on the carrion of our lives.
There where the mountains break and fall
the city dreams a fatal song.

2

The castle at the end of the curled road
sings fado. The pale trees weep leaves,
offering embrace to stone.
I become the voice I hear.

3

The lemon tree by the window wears
two birds. The birds are not singing.
I listen to their song.
Why is the fountain crying?

4

The woman in the bus who sang
sang softly of our long delay.
We were going nowhere.
I drank the song the woman sang.

5

You were as strange as love.
The fado bar was empty,
except for all of us.
There in Coimbra, I listen.

[I hardly need explain that Rita here misrepresents me
badly. (Not to mention her inability to live in either the
present or the past.) I had delivered a package of
documents to a wine merchant in Oporto and while there
decided I would take the train south to Coimbra, largely
because I was told of a shop that had on sale some rare
green tiles. It was not my intention to listen in on any fado.
I might add that by the time I got to the tile shop the
objects of my little quest were gone.]

$[$hornbook #46$]$

[Kleinhart was a compelled poet. She disappeared into art.]

Raymond, she told me one afternoon while we were eating ripe peaches on the deck outside her kitchen door, if urine came forth as song, you'd still manage to remain silent.

Give me a little credit, I said. At least I try not to be a poet.

I asked her what she looked for in a man and she said she looked for signs of fair play. Pass me that knife, she added. She had a way of splitting a peach with a knife, then removing the stone. I prefer to eat the stone free of the sweet-smelling flesh.

She had a way of remembering everything I made the mistake of saying. Men can't talk, she liked to tell me. Let me tell you about it, I said, trying to see her through the screen door that opened onto the deck. I had stepped into the kitchen to find a bottle opener. She snapped a picture of me through the screen.

Rita fancied herself a recluse. She lived alone in her ranch house and leased the land to neighboring ranchers. The mailman once told me when I asked him if he had seen her leave that the mailbox where her driveway joined the road was sometimes stuffed full to overflowing before she deigned to empty it.

When I complained, licking the peach juice from the
fingers of my right hand, that she almost never wrote me a
letter, she explained that she allowed herself to write one
letter and one only each week, no matter what urgencies
might surround her.

Embrace, I suggested. Not surround.

Surround, she said.

> He is become the belled cat,
> I the mouse, rosy and fat.

[hornbook #47]

This hornbook bears the subtitle, Exhibit A. In the middle
of an otherwise rational poem she speculates:

> When one has had one's say, assay
> or not at all the bed to climb
>
> Do not attend the buttoned if
> of once and then the truly stiff
>
> The lowly page and laughter rhyme
> the pubic tale itself bewray
>
> The tousled straw with love acquaint
> the tasseled town a red to paint

We recognize in these unlikely lines her wish to erase herself from the literary scene. She is, here, as good as gone. A goner. She abjures sense as we think we know it. She tells us there is another possibility in language and she is on her way to asking what it is. She adds on a postcard apparently intended for herself but never mailed, Some days poetry is a dialogue with nobody.

Raymond, she assured me, when I inquired about the Exhibit A thing, there is more than meets the eye standing between well hung and well hanged.

[hornbook #57]

I suppose it's time I commented on Rita's famous little verse that the literary folk like to refer to as "I'm So Glad You Called":

> I'm so glad you called, asshole, the house was
> pleasantly quiet before the phone rang and you
> tried to say hello, hello, you said, as if even
> the door frame should remember your final
> goodbye. Hey, goodbye. I'm so glad you called.

Hardly an auspicious opening. I wish someone would praise me for my ironic reply:

> O once my heart was full of joy
> But now it's full of song instead.
> Who was it wronged this singing boy?
> What was it done me wrong in bed?

And why is it that only pain can make us burst into words?
Did Rita trump up her occasional rejections of me just so
that I might be given the power of speech?

We went head to head as poets, she and I, there's no
denying it. She was into that willful stuff. The old forms
were good enough for me, and on occasion I now take one
of her poems and give it the look it should have by
highlighting in her disorder an iamb or two.

What small perversions of the body make us sing? Tickled
in the groin, we giggle poems.

> The aging apple and the angled ached.
> O blaggard laggard line, indeed. Opaque.

[hornbook #51]

Let's be honest. What could she possibly see in me? And
let me answer my own question before you make a wrong
guess. She saw in me the aging lover who made her ever
young. She saw in me the silence that must speak itself by
quoting her. She heard in me tra-la tra-la.

As poets we attribute to ourselves the poems we record on
paper. The presumption of the poet is one of technology's
petty triumphs.

Should we not say that every poem is "attributed" to the poet named in small print under the title? What rapacious need makes the poet claim the multitude by the small ordering of a signature?

Does it not take a bundle of texts, a blather of lives, to tumble one poem out of one acquisitive poet?

Poetry is excrement, a discharge of the body. It is marginally useful as fertilizer. In using it as fertilizer we run the risk of transmitting a variety of venereal diseases.

Rita Kleinhart saw in me the klutz who might bumble her obscurity into the annals—is analetic a word?—of that morbidity we call literature.

What torpor is it that enables the poet to drowse a few scratches onto the beauty of a white page?

Is not the elegance of almost any naked ass to be preferred to the puffy regurgitation of accumulated consonants?

Kick a dong of lickpence,
A belly full of blear.

Enough repression. It is high time we got down to the text.

[hornbook #**52**]

I wonder sometimes if Rita is in this house where I, in her absence, am supposed to be ordering her papers. What if her apparent disappearance was a clever way of getting me into her home?

Sometimes, late at night, I swear I hear footsteps. Poetry is a radical form of stealth. What does that make of the poet?

Sometimes, I swear, her papers, come morning, are not exactly where I left them the previous night. Something I could not track down late at night is there in the morning, obvious, staring me in the face.

To take poetry into one's hands is to take one's own life into one's hands. Surely Rita understood this when she asked me, late one evening, if I would, should the occasion arise, organize her papers and have them deposited in the vaults of the University of Calgary Special Collections Library. When I told her next morning that, yes, I would be happy to make her remains secure, she asked me what I was talking about.

Hornbook #52 makes mention of a ghost that Rita claimed was somehow herself; when she caught glimpses of its presence in her sprawling house, there on the edge of the Battle River coulees, she had the sensation that the ghost, not she, was Rita Kleinhart.

Why do I listen so intently in the dark, to the small winds that walk up out of the river valley? One midnight I woke with a start at the touch of a hand to my throat, and found the hand to be my own. We are never safe from ourselves, never. We stave off the marauder, the marauder who writes the poem, by writing the poem.

$$\left[\,\text{h o r n b o o k}\ \text{\#}24\,\right]$$

Sometime, Rita said, I want to go all the way up to the treeline.

We were hiking together, into the bare, south-facing coulee hills in the western part of her ranch. I helped her take off her hiking boots and her socks. I kissed the blisters on the bottoms of her toes. She was wearing a denim skirt. As I knew on my lips the changing taste of her sweat I knew I had strayed from her toes to her ankles, then from her ankles to the backs of her knees, then to her inner thighs. She said, at the edge of my hearing, All I can see is empty sky.

Lying on my belt buckle, facing east, all I could see was the bush of her body. Bush, I whispered.

$\big[$ h o r n b o o k #**81**$\big]$

antiquarian apes arrange ancestors
bees brush berries' bosoms
crimped clowns cuddle catastrophes

These obvious lines are to be found in a heap of notes that
finally became Hornbook #81. These lines did not make
their way into the poem. She alphabetized on at length:

dutiful dotards delight dowagers
entrancing enemas entertain enemies
farthest friends forget favors

One cannot help but detect a message even in scraps so
random as these doodled lines. I am hardly to be judged
paranoid if I hear in these fragments a foredooming of my
simply joy. Rita loved to hate me. Forgive the cliché, but
there it is, and the devil take the hindmost, what are words
but unavoidable accidents? You must practice, she told me,
and this in no uncertain terms, to confound the possibility
of your encountering your own double.

$\left[\text{hornbook } \#82\right]$

You are what remains after night's fall.
You are what remains after nights fail.

I check her phone bills for calling card charges, then pay up
out of my own pocket, since most of the calls are
apparently my own. I try to remember her last words, there
in the museum in Frankfurt. We had not spoken for a
considerable time before I turned to break the silence and
found she was not there at my side.

Perhaps she said to me, You should drink your apple juice,
it will relieve your anxieties about your bowel movements.
But that was before I fell into my sulk, and I had, yes, fallen
into a little sulk; but she knew I liked my times of quiet,
times inevitably followed by chatter and stark need.

Perhaps she said to me, How can you do this, travel for a
living, entering into languages of which you do not
understand a word? But those were not her final words,
she would not have let the matter rest there, be assured.
We were having an early breakfast at an outdoor restaurant
in front of a row of restored houses, in some sort of a
square, and at the time we were talking about architecture.
You are the prisoner of space, not I, Raymond. And please,
if nothing else, I beg you, drink your apple juice.
I think she had something more to say. We marched off in
silence together toward the renowned museum.

It is in Hornbook #82 that she writes:

Final words are as good a place as any;
having begun, we dare to begin.

As I say, and let me repeat, I cannot for the life of me recall
what her final words might have been. She did send
postcards that day, the day of her celebrated
disappearance. But none to me. And did she perchance
have the cards written and addressed before she conned
me into a petty little disagreement about who is the
prisoner and of what, and how does a shared language do
anything but seal tight the door on its rusty hinges? Rap
rap, we say, knocking our knuckles red. Hello? Is there
anyone home?

That her house has only a minimal attic is a shame; even a
ghost in Rita Kleinhart's attic would find itself homeless.

$\big[$ h o r n b o o k **#82** $\big]$

Some days I have nothing to do, I once told Rita, and can't
find the time to get it done.

Sometimes, Rita replied, waking up in the morning is like
falling asleep.

That is why I do not now believe she disappeared when she
disappeared. By her lascivious feigning she turned me into
the merest lackey who must propagate her poems.

> He, the drear and monkey-slave of time;
> she, eternal spinner of sublime.

> He, scrawny, the dancer at her feet;
> she the grinder grinding out the beat.

> She continuous, like god, or scat,
> sets him upon the ground to pass her hat.

Let me, my dearest dear, add my own two cents' worth.
One would like to assume that even a poet, a poet feigning
death, a poet proclaiming the untoward liberty of her
poems, might recollect the oblong press of desire.

> Tickle tickle little tum.
> How I wonder where you bum.

So there.

Who says my poems are poems?
My poems are not poems.
After you know my poems are not poems,
Then we can begin to discuss poetry.

—RYOKAN

THE KYOTO

MOUND

[hornbook #**55**]

We turn to speak and confront an absence. Thus we become, all of us, poets.

When the two RCMP officers came to the ranch house door, here on the edge of a steep coulee, I assumed they had come to inquire after Rita Kleinhart. It turned out they had come at her request.

Rita, by fax from Kyoto, had insisted those two intruders interrupt their highway patrol and pay a visit to her ranch. I was making myself a pot of coffee when they pounded on the front door.

How did she know you would find me here? I inquired of the inquirers.

Come with us, Raymond, the law replied, speaking its single voice.

I said (we surrender variously), I will not.

Then they added, again in their deep complicity: She wonders if she killed you. She would like to know if you are dead.

Her poems, I said, long ago condemned me to death. Would you care for a cup of coffee?

Those two uniformed policemen fled as if they had met a ghost.

[hornbook #56]

I have lived so long in the world that everything has already happened.

How, Rita, having disappeared, do you find a balcony from which to dispute my presence in this clumsy apparatus that is our stretch of days?

We have made a small trade, you and I. I occupy your abandoned house. Therefore, by your crystal logic, it is I who am missing from the world, not you. But surely it is, always, the poet who is absent from the terrors of existence, not the reader.

[hornbook #90]

I quote you to yourself:

A poem is the hypotenuse that lovers dream.
A poem is a logbook.

[h o r n b o o k #78]

Raymond, it is the unpredictable that makes for the poem.
That is why I am in Kyoto. I like the signs that I cannot read.
Why do I call them, for lack of a better word, profound?

Some mornings I go to the garden behind my favorite
Shinto shrine and walk across the pond by stepping from
stone to stone. This morning I closed my eyes and
managed four steps before I peeked.

[h o r n b o o k #34]

In Hornbook #34 you make mention of "the kiss that
sprouts a tongue" (a grotesque image, don't you think?),
this in a context that suggests that love is not a departure
at all but rather a kind of invasion:

> The kiss that sprouts a tongue . . . [etc., etc.],
> this and the hanged head . . . [etc., etc.]
> catastrophe and corpse together . . . cause.

I leave your platitudes to your own imagination. You
wanted me dead. Only the death of love gives more
passion to the poet than does the love of death. [I once
remarked to Rita (we were seated on the deck of her ranch
house; we were holding hands): I am at most a guest, at
best a ghost. At best a ghost aghast, she emended.]

You are in a tight corner, there in all of Japan.

$\Big[\text{h o r n b o o k } \#\mathbf{13}\Big]$

We come, Rita, we come to apostrophe. We turn away to make address to whom or what we would address. But is that not always the predicament of both poet and poem?

I intended to compose a WANTED poster and circulate it on Internet, only to find that what I had to say owed much to your own cryptic hornbooks:

> somewhere out there
> the fence is down

I entered your abandoned house as I enter your abandoned poems, lovingly. I had proposed to write a description and put it into circulation in the expectation of bringing you back. Why then did your precious policemen come to find, not us, but me?

> How might the berry leave the bush
> but in the bird's belly?
> Poetry, now, is a chokecherry breakfast.
> It squirts the eye a purple hue.

$\big[$ h o r n b o o k #20$\big]$

Raymond, let me continue what I was about to say—when
I turned to you there in a darkened room in the Frankfurt
Museum of Modern Art and found that you had vanished.
Yours is the pathos of the aging male. You think that now
that your life is spent you have lived a full life—and arrived
at wisdom. [Rita, please—no more woodcuts of Japanese
courtesans turned into postcard revelations at a discount
price.] And by the way, Raymond, life tonight is a sushi bar
and a bottle of beer and a glass of sake and the touch of a
knee against a thigh.

You loathe your own niggling mind, and well you should.
You should have been born in Roman times, and assigned
to harvest an abandoned field of barley on a surrendered
frontier.

$\big[$ h o r n b o o k #32$\big]$

It's hard to tell. The poet's worn-out truth
It's hard to tell the worn-out poet's ruth.

[The poet is the criminal, the reader
sleuth.]

[hornbook #79]

I have become a collection of rectangular sheets of
Japanese paper, some of those sheets figured with cranes
and chrysanthemums, some with wavering red lines that
avoid meeting, some with maple leaves like scars on what
might be flowing water, some with the messages of lovers
(I think) almost bruised into the paper itself.

(Did I mention that I'm here in Kyoto to visit my old friend
Robert? He has come to the lunatic suspicion that in a
later life he will become a Japanese monk. He is here to
study posters. He is of the opinion that nowadays a poem
should aspire to be a poster of sorts on the brick wall of
our denials.)

Here we eat seaweed.

[hornbook #17]

Somewhere in my childhood I read a poem that said

Pussycatpussycatwherehaveyoubeen?
I'vebeentoLondontoseetheQueen.

Pussycatpussycatwhatdidyouthere?
Ifrightenedalittlemouseunderachair.

And after that I was a poet.

[hornbook #62]

Think of yourself as being under arrest, Raymond. That is
the consequence of your squandering the poet's thrift.
And would you mind watering the plants in the living
room? That's all I ask of you.

Was not the handle a great invention?

[hornbook #21]

Is not the poet ever a forgery of the poem?

I found in the stack of papers I have designated The Kyoto
Mound Rita's first reference to the Japanese hermit-poet,
Ryokan. She was much fascinated that his reputation was
established after his death by his devoted loved one,
Teishin, who, it might be said, by her slavish caring gave his
small life its long endurance. [I sit at your absent feet. Here,
in front of a misted mirror, I practice bowing.]

[In that same archival deposit, Rita, you seem to imply that
I am a jealous lover. Ha. Please, spare me love's murky,
morbid triangles. Is not the you-me mishmash paste
enough?] [Who is it, ever, authors the author. So to speak.
Ahem.]

I would like to live gently in the world.

$$\left[\text{h o r n b o o k } \#74\right]$$

[You write to tell me here that there in Kyoto Robert says this and Robert says that. Your friend Robert, he does love his theories, doesn't he? You tell me that now he realizes that a poem is a fractal. I preferred him way back when he argued, in a fit of blinding lucidity, that a poem is a poem. By the same token he then claimed that you cannot say what you mean, you can only say what you say. Fair enough, I would say.]

Poet, no thyself.

[To comment further and even more succinctly: It strikes me that Rita sees in Japan what she aspires to as a poet. She sees Japan as a way of using everything toward originality rather than a way of working from originality toward everything. She would seem to forget that the Japanese worked from a confusing state of ruin, not from the bright promise of happiness that was (and is, and remains) my offering.]

[hornbook #24]

We come to the end of autobiography. Our lives
abandon us.

We are bemused by traces that suggest that once we wrote
poems. Here in Kyoto I become one of the signs that I
cannot read.

If you can't find me you know where I am.

We are always, and never ever, end even then, the same.

Our lives choose other genres.

Why do I feel such sorrow when I feel joy?

[hornbook #26]

It is the usurping reader who sets the poet free to
write again.

Today is always today. The quest for immortality is a
symptom of the poet's constipatory inclination. Soft drink
machines eat coins and shit cans.

Old sniffysnaff himself, the boggy reader, entertained by
unexpected recurrences and all the consoling rejuvenation
inherent in absolute ruin.

The text as empty as a temple. Kyoto, to my surprise, is an industrial city. There on the way up to the temple's gate I stopped to buy three masks. I gave all three to a beggar.

$$\Big[\text{h o r n b o o k } \text{\#}50\Big]$$

Love, that fatal pharmacy.
A choice of remedies: the (fatal) poem.

What I wanted was to be a poet of the floating world. But I didn't know that until I came here to Kyoto. Here in Kyoto one morning I stopped to eat an orange and did not get to the temple.

You think that poems are a longing for an end.

The Calgary Trail

MOUND

$\big[$ h o r n b o o k #**1**$\big]$

Often in the afternoon he cries for awhile. He wants a
poem that will be as accommodating as a peanut shell.
Sometimes he sits at his desk while he cries. Sometimes he
goes outside and pretends he is weeding his rock garden.
He wants a poem that will make him understand why men
plant land mines.

Sometimes he laughs in the middle of his crying. He wants
his fingers to recover their lost intelligence. He wants his
mouth to speak. He stares out through the windows at the
place where the sky should be. He wants a brick to crash
through one of the windows, a brick thrown by a poem.

[hornbook #95]

If we are ever going to walk from Edmonton to the invention of south, we had better get started. I'm not saying it's a long walk. We won't be surprised by the sudden appearance of herds of buffalo. Or of deserts or, for that matter, of the occasional palm. What I'm suggesting is, winter might arrive in early fall.

Edmonton is a city of edges. Winter has an edge to it. So, for instance, does the wind. At least at certain times of the year. Poetry is like that too. I mean, poetry is like the North Saskatchewan River, it makes its way, indirectly, toward tundra and polar bears. All this in the habit of sea level. All this for the inscription of ice.

[hornbook #33]

After the line went plop
poetry came to a stop.

This burgeoning by disparity and apperception. This blind butting. This holophrastic hey.

After the head began to swell
the poet's body went to hell.

The sun comes up and the sun goes down. You may have noticed.

[hornbook #96]

Poets in southern Alberta look at and even listen to
sunflowers as prayer wheels. They rustle in a chinook wind
of any consequence whatsoever. That is, the prayer wheels
do. Rustle, I mean. Or is it the sunflower leaves? Or is it the
poets themselves? That rustle. Since they live in southern
Alberta. Ha. Well, anyway. Ignore the consequence
business. It was not my intention to raise that issue. What
I'm trying to say is, thank our lucky mantra for fields of
sunflowers.

[hornbook #5]

What if ornament is the sole remainder of our each
intention?

At least I am increasing the range of my blindness.
Consider Robert himself, the merest trace in my poems.

> I have so long ago the ghost up given
> Kick and a run us ride we now til day
> So lone so lean, up giving now the ghost
> To where, a house or call, a coursing home.

[hornbook #88]

Because the path fizzled out at the cliff's edge.

$\left[\text{h o r n b o o k } \#\mathit{28}\right]$

A poem is an empty house.

[Stranger, you must enter, then knock.]

In a poem, everything (including the hollow door, the reddening sky) is at risk. A risking business:

once again the old thump
onto belly or the rump.

$\left[\text{h o r n b o o k } \#\mathit{27}\right]$

The crescendo of our loneliness fills library basements. Books transform into dust, dust into landfills, landfills into gas. There is always hope.

The brittleness of our desire forces us to climb stairs on our hands and knees. We groan. We imagine we are praying. There is always hope.

He is always standing in the snow, watching for the sun.

$$\Big[\text{h o r n b o o k } \#2\Big]$$

Traceries of the finite are so indelible.

He starts a fire in the barbecue pit, sending up a column of smoke. See, I am not here. If you seize what I mean.

He finds in the cellar her jars of canned plums and mustard pickles and rhubarb jam. She is a poet, and therefore must return.

He waits for the triangulation that will tell him how far she is from speaking. He waits for the spoken word that might erase the need for the poem.

$$\Big[\text{h o r n b o o k } \#25\Big]$$

Tattletale, tattletale,
hanging on a bull's tail.

Don't ask why I'm hoarse,
said the cow.

Hey, I said.
Straw's cheaper.

Well? I said.
A hole in the ground, you replied.

Our nostrum
whose art is nostrum.

$\Big[$ h o r n b o o k #9 $\Big]$

The poem is always stating its own poetics. All I can add is
that one time years ago while I was trying to rob a crow's
nest I chanced to realize that if I was ever to get to the top
of the tree I would first of all have to find boots or running
shoes that were suitable to such versions of climbing and
pants that would not slip up into the crack of my ass or
down off my hips in a manner or manners that might cause
unintended damage to the wearer and to the tree and to
the crow alike. I might add further that one time while I
was trying to snare a gopher by placing a noose made of
binder twine over a gopher hole and then carefully pouring
a bucket of water into the hole I quite by accident dumped
the water into the boot on my left foot and almost
simultaneously caught the ankle of my right leg in the
aforementioned noose. There was, at that time, a bounty
offered by the municipality on gopher tails and crows'
eggs. The crow's eggs of which I have made mention
hatched, to the best of my knowledge, into healthy and
hungry young crows. The gopher escaped unharmed.

Vanished without a trace, the poem begins.

[h o r n b o o k #91]

Poet and/or poem: varieties of equilibrium.

> Finding a lover is a false start.
> Fibrillations of the pitipat heart.
> The search for truth is a bum steer.
> It's much more likely we're looking for beer.
> What can I possibly rhyme with mud?
> Is "pod" close enough? Or "good"?
> It is the sentence that (sometimes) thinks.
> All the rest is twats and dinks.

[h o r n b o o k #63]

> You cannot persuade me that poetry is the cause of poetry.
> But maybe it is.

[Rita, sometimes when I'm sitting here alone in your house, watching a hockey game on a Saturday night, I hear the back door open. I hear the door close again. I hear the lock. I feel just the slightest gust of cold air. Where are you?]

[hornbook #92]

P.S. Or to put it another way, I am suggesting that simply by writing the words "Once upon a time" and then attempting to complete the sentence we are launched into novels, into paleontology, into myth and astronomy and gossip. . . . And that reminds me, whatever did you do with my copy of *Mother Goose?*

[hornbook #80]

Nothing is as important as nothing.

I find this one-sentence poem a puzzler. You told me late on a January night over scotch and a drop or two of melted snow that the idea of zero was only introduced into Western thought (from India, I believe you said) in the twelfth century. You wondered how that introduction altered our ability to commence the writing of a poem. Did that same question send you on your fool's errand around this nought that is our globe? [And by the way, don't be fooled: the world is flat. Consider a sheet of paper.] I might add that you gave me a blank look while raising the question. Then you added, smiling your mischievous smile: The poem must zero in. Terrific. [Where are you tonight?] But why should the poem be hieroglyphic? I would argue: the poem must matter; the poem must scatter. [Ha.] [Sometimes I feel uncertain about uncertainty itself.] [Hee.] And [Ho.]: Why are poems, like wine glasses and poisons, kept high on a shelf?

$\big[$hornbook #$[$ b l a n k $]$ $\big]$

Knowledge is insufficient. Why else would I throw sand in your eyes?

These tidbits (concatenations) from Rita's table become, for me, the prize.

[Rita, sometimes my back is sore. Sometimes my nuts ache. Sometimes I hear the empty rooms of your house talking to each other. Why am I always coming to the limits of poetry? The poem as bronchial wheeze. The sickness of the poet. The featherless arms that fail in flight. The toes that are hooked into clay. The goodbye poet who never leaves the crypt of eternal self-love. The farting poet who thinks he has heard a song. Poet, if can't grow up, at least grow down. Become a carrot, a parsnip. Even a potato. Let the earth conceal your shame. You mistook the mushrooms in your head for truth. Celebrate the actual beauty of mushrooms. Rejoice in their improbabilities. Accept the shortness of the season. Accept the shortness of your own breath. If you cannot suffer light, learn to engender in the dark. The poem as hacking cough, as a croaking in the larynx, as a green discharge from blackened lungs. Poet, if you propose to make poems out of your halloween existence, you must learn to shit pumpkins.]

Dear Raymond. You are lost in your own prologue. Get a life.

P.S., Could you possibly meet me in _____?

[hornbook #11]

anchor	bottle	crazy	
doodle	entrance	fondle	gargoyle
	handle	imprint	jester
kibitz		laggard	mustard
	number		
		ogle	
potter	query		rusted
sorrow		tunnel	ulcer
	vector	whittle	
x-rated	yodel		ziggurat

ROBERT KROETSCH

$\left[\text{h o r n b o o k \#[ ]}\right]$

One of the considerable and neglected art forms is the stack of papers.

This can be at once a literary form and a version of performance art. In my own case it takes the form, most often, of a stack of letters which I feel I should or must answer quite soon. But not immediately. The stack then occasions in me a complex mixture of delay, anticipation, dread, shame, guilt and self-condemnation. I am vaguely aware of the individual sheets of paper and texts in the stack, but the hole [sic] is much greater than the sum of the parts. The mere and sustained appearance of the stack, unfortunately, announces a kind of completion. It is a completion which is flexible in that it can be added to but not subtracted from. The stack, like a poem, begins, if nothing else, to describe intention.

$\left[\text{h o r n b o o k \_\_?}\right]$

What is poetry but a resistance to its own urgency?

The body is. The body does.
The rest is all a vague because.

[Rita, your rhubarb patch is both drug and tang. And yet I prefer, for breakfast, the puckering taste of chokecherry. These coulee hills of yours, even now, are creased with scented blossoms. I beg you, let me eat where I will.]

It is tough enough describing ice.
Just try describing paradise.

[hornbook #97]

Travel is only a departure. Its name announces an
unwillingness to arrive.

    Yes, I will meet you in _____.
    I will be there.
    You will recognize me by the smile
    I'm trying not to wear.

Each line of poetry surrounds itself with what remains
unvisited. Writing a poem is like helping a wobbly old man
onto a streetcar that is starting to move.

[hornbook #18]

The lurching diaphragm outlines the poem. In the hard up
and down of its forgetfulness it composes Homer and all
the seas he sailed. It composes Sappho's arms. Her warm
belly and her damp thighs.

[the Raymond himself hornbook]

Rita Kleinhart is afraid of chokecherry juice:
she claims it sometimes tastes of blood.

She is also afraid of potted geraniums
and blisters. Not to mention grand pianos.

She is afraid of the shadow that casts a dog.
She is afraid of the voice of an empty room.

What is a poem but an answer to fear?

Rita Kleinhart is afraid of nothing.
She says so herself.

THE RK HORNBOOK

RETRACTIONS

Archivist's Note: This bare assemblage constitutes those few drafted but not completed hornbooks that do not seem to accord with Rita's own poetic intentions. I am led to suspect that her conversations with me, over the years, on those occasions when we had the good fortune to share small intimacies, led her to doubt her own rather stoutly held convictions. Rather than place my own name in the summary title, I have chosen to call these sometimes hesitant poems "The RK Hornbook Retractions." By this strategy I give full acknowledgement to Rita and at the same time note her uniquely perspicacious if somewhat sulky disagreements with herself.

$\left[\text{h o r n b o o k } \textbf{A}\right]$

I feared she had entered infinity.
Her eyes refused all diagrams of horizon.

And yet, to rescue language from the infinite
was her first intention. Accordingly,
she set out. I had hoped she would
take me along. You know. A friend.
A companion. Maybe even a lover.

She could smell the farthest galaxy.
Was it heat or cold that gave her direction?

$\left[\text{h o r n b o o k } \textbf{B}\right]$

February is composed entirely of white iron.
In the white cold heat of a February moon,
poets warm themselves with four-line stanzas.
They freeze their tongues to doorknobs.

Politicians distribute promises
to the homeless; white rabbits too
paint themselves no color, betrayed,
if at all, by the merest track. Or turd.

One is tempted, vaguely, to hope
that hell might be a realizable fiction.
Except that colder than the hobs of same,
in prairie talk, ain't under interdiction.

Fame is a raw and dripping nose
of no allowable consequence.
Farmers unbale their hay.
Famine and the rent come due

warily, like deer to feedlots,
as if the tight gun itself might be frozen.
Snowblowers howl in the darkness.
They cannot persuade, and quit.

Daybreak, such as it is,
is a pale surrender to stillness.
Even bankers cannot imagine gold.
Magpies hardly manage to shit.

Dogteams and rich Italian tenors
try to crack open the timid sky.
The one clean sheet is a sheet of ice.
And no one utters that cold word, nice.

$\Big[$hornbook $\mathbf{C}\Big]$

This is a shaky proposition, but: let's give it a try: Poetry
is a changing of the light.

Just this morning, for instance, while listening to the
rhythms of your breathing,

I noticed the outline of a window behind the thin red curtain,
then a sort of oak desk or table under the window,
then your plain white panties on the floor by the bed.

We write down words, thinking they will instruct us.

[In this poem we hear a direct reference to the function of
the hornbook as a teaching device. That I, Raymond, was
not the surrogate author of this poem, fills me with a
sadness that borders on lamentation. The curtains in my
too-small bedroom are a subtle green.]

$\left[\text{h o r n b o o k } \textbf{D}\right]$

Getting here is our only story.
Talk about pissing up a rope.

Why do live poets gather
empty aluminum cans?

Ours is a world bloodied
by a kiss—or ketchup.

P.S., Wear shades after sundown.
Do not peer in at open windows.

$\left[\text{h o r n b o o k } \textbf{E}\right]$

Against reason:

You slid down the hill and laughed.
Later that same afternoon a cat's silver bell
turned into a round green boulder
and went on ringing.

I was kept busy
arranging pitch black watermelon seeds
on the sloped heights of your buttocks.

It's a brave poet
who counts her own toes.

$\begin{bmatrix} \text{h o r n b o o k } \textbf{F} \end{bmatrix}$

We are all lonely. We like to announce it.
I raise my loneliness like a dry
laurel wreath. Like a yellow plastic
mushroom. Like a green tomato.

What is the myth of the undone?
Where did I leave my other
glove? And yet, because of it
(the missing glove, the myth),
I am not quite, ever, alone.

Just the other morning, for example,
I had a chat with a woodpecker.
I was under the pile of leaves
In your garden by the walk.

$$\begin{bmatrix} \text{h o r n b o o k } \mathbf{G} \end{bmatrix}$$

We are fooled by the map.
Because of the map
we are tricked into setting out.

Because of the map
we pack extra socks and bandages
into the extra shoes we will never wear.

We are always setting out, as if
to discover where the map ends
will allow us to begin.

$$\begin{bmatrix} \text{h o r n b o o k } \mathbf{H} \end{bmatrix}$$

What is the poem but an echo of itself, a sound
we do not hear until it is gone?

The poet is merely a hillside barn,
a stone façade in an empty street,
possibly a canyon wall

returning the sound

returning the sound

returning the sound

returning the sound

$\left[\text{h o r n b o o k } \mathbf{I}\right]$

Both misers and musicians all, we count,
trusting by accident to find a poem.

Last night I tried with fingers five (or one)
to count the storied stars; and almost done

I thanked the droopy cloud that took away
the blinking lights. But then to my dismay

the poem too was gone, the night was old,
and this is all that I had left to say.

The RED SHALE

Hornbooks

[the caution hornbook]

This dark pool here
is from an old blockage
of the stream's course.

There will be no attempt
at rescue.

[hornbook for a young poet]

Have bacon (four strips,
preferably) and eggs (two, sunnyside up),

hash browns with ketchup,
toast (white) with real strawberry jam,

a glass of orange juice (small will do),
and three cups of black coffee;

then mark one of the following
(please, not with an X):

a) Tune-up and body-tone clinics are available
at reasonable prices.

b) We do have to believe in something
(don't we?).

c) We proceed by heresies, yet intend
to get to where we are going.

d) Appetite will be the end of us.

ROBERT KROETSCH

[the inspiration hornbook]

You of the almighty zap,
Zeusifer, loose and zany,
let me sizzle on your throne
for maybe forty-eight seconds;
I've had enough of your poetry crap,
just give me the last word of this poem.

[the melancholia hornbook]

The usual robins leave their broken nests and take to the
soggy sky. Geese drop by to foul the final golfers'
expensive shoes. Who could feel lonesome? Who? Even if
there is no one with whom to recite old stories and mutter
imprecations.

x

We in the back seat, and no one driving. You know. The
morning sun that morning, after one more kiss, was a red
shale red. And then it was too late. The crows had begun
their discordancies. Everywhere we listened we could hear
the dissolution of possible conjunctions.

x

The harmonies of time are few enough. Maybe it's only the year that's on its last legs. One time we hiked all the way to Lake Winnipeg, then back again. We had started at Lake Winnipeg. Actually, we set out on a summer afternoon to watch the build of thunder. It was intention that prevented us from realizing our intention.

x

But to speak again of this spring evening, the one I have not yet mentioned. The blackbird, the only one with a yellow head, is perched on a cattail at the edge of a marsh. The blackbird's head, you venture, is the sun. I hardly give it a second thought. But then you ask: Or is the sun a yellowheaded blackbird?

x

Perhaps those claws we found were once clenched toes. Even a landscape of neglect betrays intention. Consider this as speculation: we who are not here are here, and here we are not. So there is everywhere; the crocus rides the bone, the bone the crocus. Why is every poem a study in its own repetitions?

x

I awaken to a lullaby. Ceres becomes puffed rice or corn
flakes. Ceremonies of the cerebrum: we think we think,
and therefore think we were, or soon will be. The
harmonies of time are few enough. I sprinkle sugar on my
day. We eat what we are. I cross my legs and raise my
coffee cup. Somewhere else a war is exploding, an ocean
crushes its own bed.

x

Green here is and lovely
though the rain oh the rain
and days so long they will soon be short.

What after all is a poem
but a longing for a possible
reality?

x

I dab spilled coffee out of the saucer's indifference. We put
on the weather we will wear, at least until noon, then turn
off the radio and listen. If only truth had a language. If only
my raincoat had not shrunk in the dryer.

x

The elbow is a form of decisiveness, however much it
bends. Stone is insufficient: it wears itself blank in the
prophesied weather. But the elbow. Raising the cup. The
elbow, in its bending, assists in raising the anticipated cup.

x

Attunement of one's feet to the bald and hairy earth.
Consider the blackbird, perched on a reed, a north wind
blowing, the water torn. Now is the poem's beginning,
even at this late hour in the span of everywhere. Consider
the lovers, with not enough arms for all their need to
embrace. Or, if you prefer, consider the madness of wars,
the impossible weight of oceans. And even if we had been
there, would we have laughed or cried?

[hornbook #73]

When I tell you
that I love you
I am trying to tell you
that I love you.

[the mound hornbook]

A hill of beans.

The pitcher, leaning,
ready to throw
an inside curve.

The heaped earth.

[the (apocryphal?) George Bowering hornbook]

Let dead adjudication die.
Abhor the arbor and the war.
Grass, in its blind conniving,
eats the ruminating cow.
The poetry of smaller cities
neither entrance now
to hell nor blunted heaven is,
but rather walks the street in rain.
Language is, and, as itself,
becomes a high noon kind of pain.*

*One wonders if George Bowering himself wrote this
hornbook, in an attempt to insert his presence into the
Rita Kleinhart canon. Mr. Bowering, like the cowbird, is not
averse to depositing an egg or two in nests various. Rita,
apparently, was attracted to a poet whose blatant disguises
could only call attention to the conspicuously concealed
self. But I can hardly believe she would so blatantly praise
deception.

[the (apocryphal?) Doug Barbour hornbook]

Tourniquet the bleeding line
with asphodels and whisky;
wire shut the gate, then caulk
with gold, and plain convictions.
Bait the highway deep with alphabet
resounders
that loose the poet's knees
and scuttle with a broken word
the ark of dead trajectories.*

*Why a person of such cryptic intent as Rita was attracted
to the poems of a sound poet is beyond the pale of my
understanding. But there you go. She would let trace alone
speak in the concentration of her poems, yet her
admiration found focus in the kinds of performance pieces
that she could never, in the mysteries (consider ark) of her
withholding, herself perform. She admired a kind of daring
that she did not herself possess.

$\big[$hornbook #**1** [revised] $\big]$

If you want to be a poet
you have to be a poet.

$\big[$hornbook #**69** $\big]$

Why is a hornbook like a hand-held
mirror?

Take a look for yourself.

$\big[$hornbook #**16** or **76** [handwriting problem] $\big]$

A shifty business this, writing the poem's
weather.

One time I saw a man hanging upside down
from a cloud. Perspective, he said, is
everything.

[the hollow hornbook]

We

Are   Were

Always   Never

Never   Always

Lonesome

Again, the hole in the middle of things. And that is the question, with poetry. The poem itself is at best a trace of what is fundamental and now is forgotten. Mere psychoanalysis will never get us there. One must attempt the impossible poem. To write what is possible is to concede victory to the unspeakable. How then give it a surface that lets the eye hear?

Or to put it another way, Rita presents to me my absence. I can only assume she wrote this hornbook intending to throw it away. Granted, every poem is a casting out, an abandonment, but Rita went too far. She loved to leave me fretting and stewing about the significance of every emptiness she was able to uncover. The poem as vacated crypt. As wound. As pothole.

$$\begin{bmatrix} \text{hornbook fragment A; or,} \\ \text{the flat earth hornbook} \end{bmatrix}$$

The four winds and the quartered earth,
the balding head at point of birth—

Rita spoke the preceding couplet out of pure inspiration—
even instinct, one might say—while she and I delighted
ourselves, secure in the intimacies of flowered percale
sheets and a down-filled quilt and heaps of pillows. I find in
this snippet not so much a poem's genesis as a poem's
shadow. Rita, in response to my moment's hesitation,
proceeded to speculate on what a mathematician had
remarked to her—that is: The flat world hypothesis
explains a great deal.

   Is that so? I murmured blindly, by way of response.

   Rita went on to quote the anonymous mathematician at
some length: While driving through the streets of a city, he
had posited as an example, the flat world theory is superior
to that of the round. While harvesting a quarter section of
wheat, a supposition of flatness will suffice. Look at a map
of the North Saskatchewan River system, which includes
the Battle River; up and down concur, without rotundity.
Yes, the notion of a round world is important if you are
Columbus, or the captain of an oil tanker. But, if you are
driving straight through from Calgary to Edmonton, or if
you are building a house, or if you are in bed—or, he
added—writing a hornbook—the flat world hypothesis
will suit you fine.

   Hmmm, I allowed, my tongue too busy for speech.

   I am falling off to sleep, Rita whispered.

   Aha.

   Aha?

   Aha. The flat world turns.

   And please don't sleep on your back, she added, as if
she hadn't heard a word I'd spoken. It makes you snore.

When I heard her key in the lock of the back door of her
ranch house, I covered my face with a volume of her
poems. I was lying on the couch in front of the TV, now
and then sipping a very small scotch. The Edmonton Oilers
were playing Ottawa. I am always waiting. She is always
returning, even when she is here.

I had only minutes before her unexpected appearance
composed for her a little poem of my own:

> Writing is a curse,
> Of course, or even worse.
> If writing isn't fun
> You should carry a gun.
> Writing is a blessing.
> It keeps both saints and devil
> Guessing.

Ray, she said, after our gentle embrace, you love your
loneliness. It protects you from self-knowledge. Hello, I
responded, by way of refutation.

[h o r n b o o k #[J]]

Rita, you are wont to write a crabbed and stubborn sentence, but this beats all. Without so much as a word you point straight through the dark and past the bend in the highway to the sign on the restaurant roof that, glowingly, says

EATS

[h o r n b o o k K]

Just this morning I phoned the International Date Line in Tonga, thinking that perhaps I had lost a day. The woman who answered reminded me that her ancestors were cannibals, not thieves.

Then she added, somewhat tartly I thought: And yours?

[syllabus for a return]

Read the parchment of the soles of your feet.
Where have you been? Why did you go there?
Why did you stay so long?

Read the lines around your eyes.
Why did you look directly at the sun, you fool?
What did you see that broke your heart?

I had been hoping to get there myself,
but, as you know, even the main road
is a kind of distraction.

[hornbook #98]

And sure enough, there it was,
not the sought-after needle, but,
to my agreeable astonishment,
the haystack in the field by the lane.

[acknowledgements]

Some of the hornbooks in this volume appeared in their present or slightly different forms in the following journals: *West Coast Line, Open Letter, Prairie Fire, Mattoid* (Australia), *The New Quarterly, Alberta Views, Canadian Literature,* and *Border Crossings.* A considerable number appeared in my book A *Likely Story: The Writing Life* (Red Deer: Red Deer College Press, 1995). A further number appeared in the chapbook "The Oviedo Hornbooks" (Oviedo: Universidad de Oviedo, 1999). "The Red Shale Hornbooks" also made their first appearance as a chapbook (Winnipeg: Pachyderm Press, 2000). I am grateful to the editors and staff of the University of Alberta Press for encouraging me to assemble a completed text.

Date Due

AUG 1 0 2007			